What Does the Bible Say About Salvation? Baptism? Church Membership?

Teacher's Edition

By
Pastor Jeremy Markle

WALKING IN THE WORD MINISTRIES

Pastor Jeremy Markle
www.walkinginthewordministries.net

What Does the Bible Say About
Salvation?
Baptism?
Church Membership?

by Pastor Jeremy Markle

Unless otherwise noted,
all Scripture quotations are from the King James Version.

Published by Walking in the WORD Ministries
www.walkinginthewordministries.net

Printed in the United States of America

ISBN: 978-0998064604

Contents

What Does the Bible Say About Salvation?

What Does the Bible Say About Salvation?

The Bible teaches us that Jesus came *"to seek and to save that which was lost"* (Luke 19:10). Because this is a stated purpose of Jesus Christ's life and ministry, we need to consider several questions to fully understand God's plan. *(Question # 1)*

First, *what does it mean to be "lost?"* John 3:16 helps explain the meaning of being lost spiritually when it says, ***"For God so loved the world, that he gave his only begotten Son, that whosoever believeth in him should not perish, but have everlasting life."*** To be "lost" is to "perish." Therefore, each person who does not have eternal life is "lost." To lack eternal life is to face eternal death, be separated from God and be in hell for all eternity (Revelation 20:11-15). Romans 6:23 says that death is the result of sin, ***"for the wages of sin is death ..."*** I John 3:4 explains more: ***"... sin is the transgression [violation] of the law,"*** and Romans 3:23 is very clear when it says, ***"for all have sinned, and come short of the glory of God."*** Each person has fallen short of God's perfection by sinning. Therefore, each person is in a lost condition and in need of God's salvation in order to avoid eternal death. *(Questions # 2, 3)*

Second, *how did Jesus Christ go about seeking and saving the lost?* Because God ***"... is longsuffering to us-ward, not willing that any should perish, but that all should come to repentance,"*** He chose to make a way of salvation through His Son, Jesus Christ (II Peter 3:9). John 3:16 says, ***"For God so loved the world, that he*** *gave his only begotten Son ...,*" and Philippians 2:8 tells us that Jesus Christ "*... being found in fashion as a man, he humbled himself, and became obedient unto death, even the death of the cross.*" Jesus Christ, being perfect as the only God-man, was the only possible payment for all of man's sin. I Corinthians 15:1-4 is very clear that the Gospel, or "good news," about salvation is "*... that Christ died for our sins according to the scriptures; And that he was buried, and that he rose again the third day according to the scriptures.*" Because of Jesus Christ's death, burial and resurrection, John 3:16-17 can promise eternal victory over eternal death when as it says, "*... that whosoever believeth in him should not perish, but have everlasting life. For God sent not his Son into the world to condemn the world; but that the world through him might be saved.*" God has made the only possible payment for salvation through Jesus Christ. "*Forasmuch as ye know that ye were not redeemed with corruptible things, as silver and gold, from your vain conversation received by tradition from your fathers; But with the precious blood of Christ, as of a lamb without blemish and without spot*" (I Peter 1:18-19). *(Questions # 4, 5, 6)*

Third, *how can someone be saved from his lost condition and have eternal life?* Ephesians 2:8-9 says, "*For by grace are ye saved through faith; and that not of yourselves: it is the gift of God: not of works, lest any man should boast.*" God says that we cannot gain salvation by ourselves. Our family, our friends, our religion, or any other good work cannot save us from our

8

sin problem. These verses are clear: salvation is only provided through God's grace and can only be received through our faith. The apostle Paul, while speaking of his salvation says; "*and be found in him, not having mine own righteousness, which is of the law, but that which is through the faith of Christ, the righteousness which is of God by faith*" (Philippians 3:9). The Bible is clear in John 3:18. "*He that believeth on him [Jesus] is not condemned: but he that believeth not is condemned already, because he hath not believed in the name of the only begotten Son of God.*" The only solution to your sin and eternal death is found in Jesus Christ's payment for your sin by trusting in Him alone for eternal life. Romans 10:9-10 says, "*That if thou shalt confess with thy mouth the Lord Jesus, and shalt believe in thine heart that God hath raised him from the dead, thou shalt be saved. For with the heart man believeth unto righteousness; and with the mouth confession is made unto salvation.*" To speak plainly, the choice for salvation is yours, but the results of your choice are out of your control. Romans 6:23 starts by saying, "*For the wages of sin is death ...*" You may stay in your sin and experience eternal death, or you may accept the last part of Romans 6:23 which says, "*but the gift of God is eternal life through Jesus Christ our Lord*" and experience eternal life. *(Questions # 7, 8, 9)*

Fourth, *how many times must an individual be saved?* Jesus Christ, while speaking to "*Nicodemus, a ruler of the Jews,*" said, "*Verily, verily, I say unto thee,*

9

Except a man be born again, he cannot see the kingdom of God" (John 3:1, 3). Jesus is clear. The requirement to get into God's kingdom for all eternity is spiritual birth. He was using the one-time act of physical birth to explain the one-time spiritual act of being saved. He then explains this truth further by saying *"Verily, verily, I say unto thee, Except a man be born of water [physical birth] and of the Spirit [spiritual birth], he cannot enter into the kingdom of God. That which is born of the flesh is flesh; and that which is born of the Spirit is spirit. Marvel not that I said unto thee, Ye must be born again"* (John 3:5-7). Jesus Christ was teaching Nicodemus that salvation is a one-time event that can be documented just as a physical birth date. He helps us understand that an individual's time of salvation is not something that can be changed or needs to be repeated. Each person who desires eternal life in God's kingdom must first have a physical birthday (have physical life), and then have a spiritual birth date (have spiritual life). John 1:12 assures us *"as many as received him, to them gave he power to become the sons of God, even to them that believe on his name."* *"For ye are all the children of God by faith in Christ Jesus"* (Galatians 3:26). When an individual is spiritually born, he is born into God's family and can never be removed. Although a child of God may rebel against his Heavenly Father by sinning, and his father-child relationship may be damaged for a time, God promises that *"if we confess our sins, he is faithful and just to forgive us our sins, and to cleanse us from all unrighteousness*" (I John 1:9). A child of God who has sinned must ask God for forgiveness for his sin in order to restore a good father-child relationship, but he never needs to ask to be part of God's family again. *(Questions # 10, 11, 12, 13)*

The final, yet equally important question is, *can anyone lose his eternal life?* Each person who has accepted Jesus Christ as his personal Savior has "*eternal life.*" This eternal life is forever and cannot be taken away. I John 5:13 says, "*These things have I written unto you that believe on the name of the Son of God; that ye may know that ye have eternal life, and that ye may believe on the name of the Son of God.*" God wants you to know that you have spiritual life and that it can never be taken from you because it is "*eternal.*" In order to help us understand more fully our security in Jesus Christ, John 1:12 says, "*But as many as received him, to them gave he power to become the sons of God, even to them that believe on his name.*" The Bible is clear--you cannot earn salvation on your own, and you cannot keep it in your own power. At salvation, God, through His power, has made you His child. Because God is almighty, no one can remove you from being part of His family. Jesus explains a believer's eternal security in John 10:27-30, when He says, "*My sheep hear my voice, and I know them, and they follow me: And I give unto them eternal life; and they shall never perish, neither shall any man pluck them out of my hand. My Father, which gave them me, is greater than all; and no man is able to*

11

pluck them out of my Father's hand. I and my Father are one." *(Questions # 14, 15, 16)*

Have you ever asked Jesus Christ to be your Savior? **Have you called upon the name of the Lord, admitting your sinful condition, and asking Him for His forgiveness by expressing your faith in His payment for your sin on the cross?** If you have not, please do not let another moment pass. Accept Jesus Christ as your personal Savior right now! *(Question #17)*

What Does the Bible Says About Salvation?

1. Why did Jesus come to the earth? (Luke 19:10)
   To seek and to save that which was lost

2. What does it mean to be lost? (John 3:16-18)
   Not have eternal life

3. Who is "lost?" (Romans 3:23, 6:23a)
   All people

4. Does God want you to be lost? (II Peter 3:9)
   No

5. Who did God send to earth to provide salvation? (John 3:16)
   Jesus Christ

6. How did Jesus pay for your sin? (Philippians 2:8, I Corinthians 15:1-4, I Peter 1:18-19)
   His death on the cross

7. What does God offer you as a gift? (Romans 6:23b)
   Eternal life

8. How can you have eternal life? (John 3:18, Ephesians 2:8-9, Philippians 3:9)
   (What) Believe   in (Who) Jesus Christ

9. How should you express your faith in Jesus Christ? (Romans 10:9-10)
    Confess with your mouth (prayer)

10. How many times must you be born again (saved)? (John 3:1-7)
    One time
    When are you born again?
    When I believe in Jesus Christ

11. What must you do to be born again (John 1:12, Galatians 3:26)
    Receive or believe in Jesus Christ

12. Whose family are you born into when you are born again? (John 1:12)
    The family of God

13. What must you do when you sin after you are God's child? (I John 1:9)
    Confess it to God

14. Can you know for sure you have eternal life? (I John 5:13)
    Yes

15. When you are one of God's sheep (children), Who holds you in His hand? (John 10:27-30)
    Jesus Christ and God the Father
    Can anyone or anything take you out of that hand?
    No

16. Can you ever lose your eternal life? (John 1:12, 10:27-30, I John 5:13)
    No

17. Please briefly write your personal testimony of when you asked Jesus Christ to be your personal Savior.

    _____
    _____
    _____
    _____
    _____
    _____
    _____
    _____
    _____
    _____
    _____
    _____
    _____
    _____
    _____

_____

_____

_____

_____

_____

_____

_____

_____

_____

_____

_____

_____

_____

_____

_____

_____

_____

_____

_____

_____

_____

_____

_____

What Does the Bible Say About Baptism?

What Does the Bible Say About Baptism?

The Bible tells us in Acts 2:41-42, *"Then they that gladly received his word [the salvation message] were baptized: and the same day there were added unto them [the apostles and church] about three thousand souls. And they continued stedfastly in the apostles' doctrine and fellowship, and in breaking of bread, and in prayers."* This passage is an historical accounting of the events on the day of Pentecost after Peter's preaching about the need for repentance from sin and salvation in Jesus Christ. These verses clearly present the pattern of salvation, baptism, and church membership. The individuals first *"gladly received his word,"* or with joy, believed the message of the Gospel. Second, they were *"baptized,"* and third, they *"were added unto the church."* (Question # 1)

Baptism always comes after salvation. Acts 8:12, while speaking about the events taking place in Samaria, says, *"But when they believed Philip preaching the things concerning the kingdom of God, and the name of Jesus Christ, they were baptized, both men and women."* Even more clearly, Philip states the order of salvation and baptism when speaking to the Ethiopian eunuch in verses 35-38, *"Then Philip opened his mouth, and began at the same scripture, and preached unto him Jesus. And as they went on their way, they came unto a certain water: and the eunuch said, See, here is water; what doth hinder me to be baptized? And Philip said, If thou believest with all thine heart, thou mayest. And he*

19

answered and said, I believe that Jesus Christ is the Son of God. And he commanded the chariot to stand still: and they went down both into the water, both Philip and the eunuch; and he baptized him.*" Philip makes it very clear that there is no saving power in water or being baptized into water. Baptism is simply a public testimony of your spiritual identification with Jesus Christ. *(Questions # 2, 3)*

In Matthew 3:13-17, we find the record of Jesus' baptism by John the Baptist. The Bible says, *"Then cometh Jesus from Galilee to Jordan unto John, to be baptized of him. But John forbad him, saying, I have need to be baptized of thee, and comest thou to me? And Jesus answering said unto him, Suffer it to be so now: for thus it becometh us to fulfil all righteousness. Then he suffered him. And Jesus, when he was baptized, went up straightway out of the water: and, lo, the heavens were opened unto him, and he saw the Spirit of God descending like a dove, and lighting upon him: And lo a voice from heaven, saying, This is my beloved Son, in whom I am well pleased.*" From the example of Jesus Christ, we can discover several important truths about baptism. First, John the Baptist recognized his personal unworthiness in comparison to Jesus Christ's perfection. He also questioned Jesus Christ about His need for baptism. Jesus' response indicated that He was not asking to be baptized because He had sin in His life. He was asking to be baptized because it was the right or righteous thing to do. Therefore, baptism does not help an individual with salvation from their sin, but rather is a public display that the individual's sins are already forgiven by God through salvation in Jesus Christ. *(Questions # 4, 5)*

Second, Jesus Christ stated that *"it becometh us to fulfil all righteousness"* (Matthew 3:13-17). Jesus was simply being obedient by being baptized. Through His obedience, we are taught that baptism is not an option for believers, but rather a command. Jesus had not and could not sin. Therefore, He would fulfill every God-given command perfectly. God desires that each new believer identify publicly with Jesus Christ through the waters of baptism. Jesus, by His humble obedience, has given us the pattern and example to follow from that time forward. *(Question # 6)*

Third, Jesus Christ made a personal decision to be baptized. Even when John the Baptist attempted to dissuade Jesus from being baptized, He was firm that it was necessary. This helps us understand that biblical baptism cannot be forced on someone, nor can baby baptism fulfill the will of God. Therefore, baptism is a personal choice to obey or disobey God's command.

Fourth, Jesus Christ was baptized in water. The Bible says that following His baptism He *"went up straightway out of the water."* Baptism is not sprinkling or pouring. Baptism is by immersion, which is being placed in the water. (The same concept is presented in Acts 8:35-38.) *(Question # 7)*

Fifth, Jesus Christ received the commendation and praise of His Heavenly Father after His obedience. This is also true for all those who follow the example of Jesus Christ and the command of God to be baptized. God is always pleased with obedience and calls disobedience sin. James 4:17 says; *"Therefore to him that knoweth to do good, and doeth it not, to him it is sin."*

Jesus Christ, in His final words on this earth, presented the command for baptism. Matthew 28:18-20 reports, *"And Jesus came and spake unto them, saying, All power is given unto me in heaven and in earth. Go ye therefore, and teach all nations, baptizing them in the name of the Father, and of the Son, and of the Holy Ghost: Teaching them to observe all things whatsoever I have commanded you: and, lo, I am with you alway, even unto the end of the world. Amen."* Jesus Christ was commanding, or commissioning, His disciples and each believer who followed their teaching, to go forth with a three-part ministry: teach all nations salvation, baptize those who are saved, and teach or disciple them in the Word of God. (This pattern was followed on the Day of Pentecost in Acts 2:41-42 and is accomplished through the local church today). *(Question # 8)*

Have you taken the first steps of obedience to God and growth in your spiritual life? The choice of baptism is yours, and only you can make it. Are you willing to publicly declare Jesus Christ as your personal Savior and your desire to "*... walk in newness of life*" by identifying with His death, burial (being placed under the water), and resurrection (being brought up again out of the water) (Romans 6:4)? *(Question # 9)*

What Does the Bible Say About Baptism?

1. Who was baptized on the Day of Pentecost? (Acts 2:41-42)
   Those who believed Peter's message about Jesus

2. When did Philip baptize the people of Samaria? (Acts 8:12)
   After they believed the Gospel of Jesus Christ

3. When did Philip permit the Ethiopian eunuch to be baptized? (Acts 8:35-38)
   After he believed in Jesus Christ

4. Does baptism have any saving or sin-cleansing power? (Matthew 3:13-17)
   No

5. Who was pleased with Jesus after He was baptized? (Matthew 3:13-17)
   God the Father

6. Why was Jesus baptized? (Matthew 3:13-17)
   To fulfill all righteousness

7. Where was Jesus baptized? (Matthew 3:13-17)
   In the Jordan River (in water)

8. Who commanded believers to be baptized? (Matthew 28:18-20)
   <u>Jesus Christ</u>

9. Have you obeyed God by being publicly baptized in water following your salvation? _____
   If yes, When? _____ Where? _____
   Are you walking in the *"newness of life?"* _____
   *Romans 6:4

What Does the Bible Say About Church Membership?

What Does the Bible Say About Church Membership?

The Bible teaches that following baptism the new believers joined themselves together, forming the first church. Acts 2:41-42 says, *"Then they that gladly received his word were baptized: and the same day there were added unto them [the church] about three thousand souls. And they continued stedfastly in the apostles' doctrine and fellowship, and in breaking of bread, and in prayers."* What then is the church, and why must it be part of a believer's life? (Question # 1)

First, Jesus Christ says in Matthew 16:18 *"... I will build my church; and the gates of hell shall not prevail against it."* Jesus Christ is the Creator and Builder of the church. It is on His authority that the church exists. The Bible says that *"Christ is the head"* of the church (Ephesians 5:22-23), and it is Jesus Christ who provides human leadership for the church (Ephesians 4:11-16). Some religions teach that the current living leader is the ultimate authority over the church. However, I Peter 5:2-4 speaks to the church leaders when it says, *"Feed the flock of God which is among you, taking the oversight thereof ... And when the chief Shepherd shall appear, ye shall receive a crown of glory that fadeth not away."* Jesus Christ is the *"chief Shepherd,"* and the human leadership is the under-shepherd. God provides human leadership for the church and warns that leadership that they will need to give an account to Him for how they have accomplished their ministry. *(Questions # 2, 3)*

Second, the Bible teaches that the church is to be one of the believer's resources for spiritual growth and protection. Ephesians 4:11-16 says, *"And he [Jesus] gave some, apostles; and some, prophets; and some, evangelists; and some, pastors and teachers; for the perfecting of the saints, for the work of the ministry, for the edifying of the body of Christ: till we all come in the unity of the faith, and of the knowledge of the Son of God, unto a perfect man, unto the measure of the stature of the fulness of Christ: that we henceforth be no more children, tossed to and fro, and carried about with every wind of doctrine, by the sleight of men, and cunning craftiness, whereby they lie in wait to deceive; but speaking the truth in love, may grow up into him in all things, which is the head, even Christ: from whom the whole body fitly joined together and compacted by that which every joint supplieth, according to the effectual working in the measure of every part, maketh increase of the body unto the edifying of itself in love."* *(Question # 4)*

It is God's plan for believers to learn God's Word from the ministries of the church and its leadership. The teachings believers learn will then assist them to do the work of the ministry and protect them from false teaching and the influence of the world. Also, it must be recognized that Hebrews 13:7, 17 warns church members when it says, *"Remember them which have the rule over you, who have spoken unto you the word of God: whose faith follow, considering the end of their conversation.*

Obey them that have the rule over you, and submit yourselves: for they watch for your souls, as they that must give account, that they may do it with joy, and not with grief: for that is unprofitable for you." The Bible says that the church leadership will have the responsibility of reporting to God as to how those under their leadership followed their leadership. Church leadership is responsible for teaching what it is biblically correct (II Timothy 2:15, Titus 2:1-15), and the believers are responsible for obeying what is taught (Acts 2:42, 46, James 1:22-25). *(Questions # 5, 6, 7)*

Third, the Bible helps us understand the importance and urgency of the church's ministry when it says "*And let us consider one another to provoke unto love and to good works: Not forsaking the assembling of ourselves together, as the manner of some is; but exhorting one another: and so much the more, as ye see the day approaching*" (Hebrews 10:24-25). If a believer is not attending his church regularly, he will not have the privilege of experiencing godly edification and teaching from other believers, and will lose the opportunity to minister to others. Also, there should be an urgency or desire for church attendance, because the "*day*" is "*approaching.*" The "*day*" that is "*approaching*" is the Lord's return. Because time is short, anticipation of the Lord's return should motivate believers to say, "*Let us hold fast the profession of our faith without wavering; (for he is faithful that promised)*" (Hebrews 10:23). *(Questions # 8, 9)*

Fourth, the Bible teaches that the primary place for human accountability for believers is the church. Galatians 6:1 says, *"Brethren, if a man be overtaken in a fault, ye which are spiritual, restore such an one in the spirit of meekness; considering thyself, lest thou also be tempted."* The church is the place for God's children, or spiritual *"brethren,"* to protect each other from the harms of sin. When the teaching of God's Word and the edification of fellow believers is not heeded, resulting in a fellow believer being *"overtaken"* by or falling into sin, it is necessary for a loving brother or sister in Christ to kindly seek to help the fallen believer *"in the spirit of meekness; considering thyself, lest thou also be tempted."* In Matthew 18:15-17, Jesus Christ says, *"Moreover if thy brother shall trespass against thee, go and tell him his fault between thee and him alone: if he shall hear thee, thou hast gained thy brother. But if he will not hear thee, then take with thee one or two more, that in the mouth of two or three witnesses every word may be established. And if he shall neglect to hear them, tell it unto the church: but if he neglect to hear the church, let him be unto thee as an heathen man and a publican."*

God's desire is that each believer be a part of a local church to help protect them from being entrapped by sin, and to help them get right with God and fellow believers when they do fall into sin. James 5:19-20 teaches that human accountability found through fellow believers helps prevent an individual from falling deeper in sin. *"Brethren, if any of you do err from the truth, and one convert him; Let him know, that he which converteth the sinner from the error of his way shall save a soul from death, and shall hide a multitude of sins."* *(Question # 10)*

Fifth, the Bible teaches the need for the local church in order that there is unity among believers. I Corinthians 12:12-27 helps us understand the unity of the church by saying *"For as the body is one, and hath many members, and all the members of that one body, being many, are one body: so also is Christ"* (vrs. 12). The passage goes on to give several illustrations about the body, such as, *"If the foot shall say, Because I am not the hand, I am not of the body; is it therefore not of the body?"* (vrs. 15) *"And the eye cannot say unto the hand, I have no need of thee: nor again the head to the feet, I have no need of you"* (vs. 21). God's desire is for unity and harmony among believers. This unity is found in humility and the cooperation of each member of the "body," or church, doing his part. *(Question # 11)*

As believers follow God's authority as the Creator and the source of leadership for the church, we have His promise that *"the gates of hell shall not prevail against it [the church]"* (Matthew 16:18). *(Question # 12)*

Are you a member of a Christ-focused church? Are you learning and growing spiritually from the leadership God has given you? Are you doing your part in participating in the ministry? If not, begin by following the example of the new believers in Acts 2:41-

42, when, "*... they that gladly received his word were baptized: and the same day there were added unto them about three thousand souls. And they continued stedfastly in the apostles' doctrine and fellowship, and in breaking of bread, and in prayers.*" *(Questions # 13, 14, 15)*

What Does the Bible Say about Church Membership?

1. What did the new believers do following their conversion and baptism? (Acts 2:41-42)
   a. They were added to the church
   b. They continued stedfastly in doctrine
   c. They continued stedfastly in fellowship

2. Who is the head of the church? (Matthew 16:18, Ephesians 5:22-23)
   Jesus Christ

3. Who provides church leadership? (Ephesians 4:11-16)
   Jesus Christ

4. Why does God want believers to be a part of a church and following its leadership? (Ephesians 4:11-16)
   "For the perfecting of the saints, for the work of the ministry, for the edifying of the body of Christ: Till we all come in the unity of the faith, and of the knowledge of the Son of God, unto a perfect man, unto the measure of the stature of the fulness of Christ: That we henceforth be no more children, tossed to and fro, and carried about with every wind of doctrine, by the sleight of men, and cunning craftiness, whereby they lie in wait to deceive."

5. What are believers commanded to do with church leadership? (Hebrews 13:7, 17)
    a. Remember them
    b. Follow their faith
    c. Consider the end of their conversation
    d. Obey them
    e. Submit to them

6. What is church leadership required to teach? (Titus 2:1-15, II Timothy 2:15)
    Sound doctrine

7. What should believers do with the church leadership's teaching? (Acts 2:42, 46, James 5:22-25)
    Continue it - obey it

8. What is the purpose of believers fellowshiping together? (Hebrews 10:24-25)
    a. To provoke unto love
    b. To provoke unto good works
    c. To exhort one another

9. What should motivate believers to edify each other in the church? (Hebrews 10:24-25)
    The coming of the Lord

10. What should believers do if another believer falls into sin? (Galatians 6:1)
    *Matthew 18:15-17, James 5:19-20
    Restore (look for repentance and restoration)
    How should that be accomplished?
    With meekness - considering oneself so as not to fall into temptation

11. What is a physical example of how believers should work together in the church? (I Corinthians 12:12-27)
    A body

12. Who protects the church from Satan? (Matthew 16:18)
    Jesus Christ

13. What did the people do after hearing the preaching of God's Word on the day of Pentecost? (Acts 2:41-42)
    a.   They received (believed) the Word
    b.   They were baptized
    c.   They were added to the church
    d.   They continued stedfastly in doctrine
    e.   They continued stedfastly in fellowship

14. Are you currently a part of a church and continuing "***stedfast***" in the teaching of God's Word and fellowshiping with other believers? (Acts 2:41-42)

_____

15. If you are not currently a member of a Bible-believing church, are you willing to join the church who is sharing this study with you? _____
If yes, please do not hesitate to talk to the pastor as soon as possible and share with him your personal testimony of salvation and baptism and desire to be a part God's program of the church by becoming a member.

Notes

Other Ministry Resources Available
From
Walking in the WORD Ministries

Marriage: A Covenant Before God presents 10 biblical studies about marriage, each one is based on the marital relationship of Adam and Eve and has the purpose of helping young couples understand God's plan and purpose for their life together. Included are practical questions, illustrations, and applications for each biblical truth in order that the couple might grow in their knowledge of each other and how they can glorify God together.

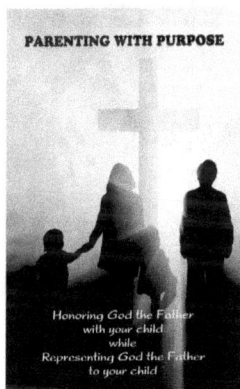

Parenting with Purpose seeks to help young parents to spiritually prepare for the great privilege they have to care for and guide the life of one of God's precious creations. The first three lessons focus on the parents' need to honor God with their child, while the final three lessons focus on the parents' opportunity to represent God the Father to their child.

The Armor of God for Your Daily Battles provides a daily Bible study to review the spiritual resources God has provided for each believer so that they can enjoy a victorious Christian life.

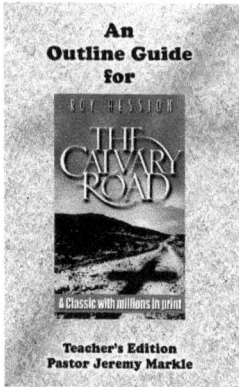

The Calvary Road: Outline Guide was written to enhance your ability to understand, remember, and apply the important spiritual truths shared by Roy Hession in his book, The Calvary Road. After reading each chapter, you can review its content by filling in the blanks, considering the additional passages provided, and answering the reflection and application questions. Throughout this outline guide there are a few special features to help you focus on the truths being taught.

Missions: Ministering Beyond Our Borders was written to provide insight into the physical, emotional, and spiritual adjustments a missionary faces as he begins his new life and ministry. Throughout its pages you will find spiritual encouragements for the missionary and helpful hints for his family and friends who desire to support him in his service to their Lord and Savior Jesus Christ. There is also "Missionary Edition" which provides a large appendix with additional tips specifically for missionaries.

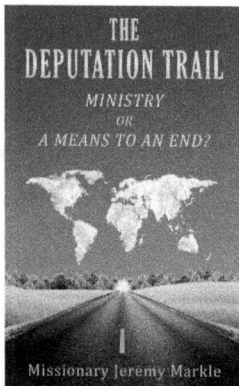

The Deputation Trail: Ministry or a Means to an End? was written to help missionaries during their pre-field ministry by presenting biblically-based philosophies and practical tips to guide them through a God-honoring, church-expanding, and believer-edifying, deputation ministry.